INSPIRE
HAIR FASHION FOR SALON CLIENTS

Salon Decaro Inc. • HAIR: Jennifer Ellis • MAKEUP: Danielle LaSalle • PHOTO: Richard Gardner

INSPIRE
HAIR FASHION FOR SALON CLIENTS

Featuring UPDOS

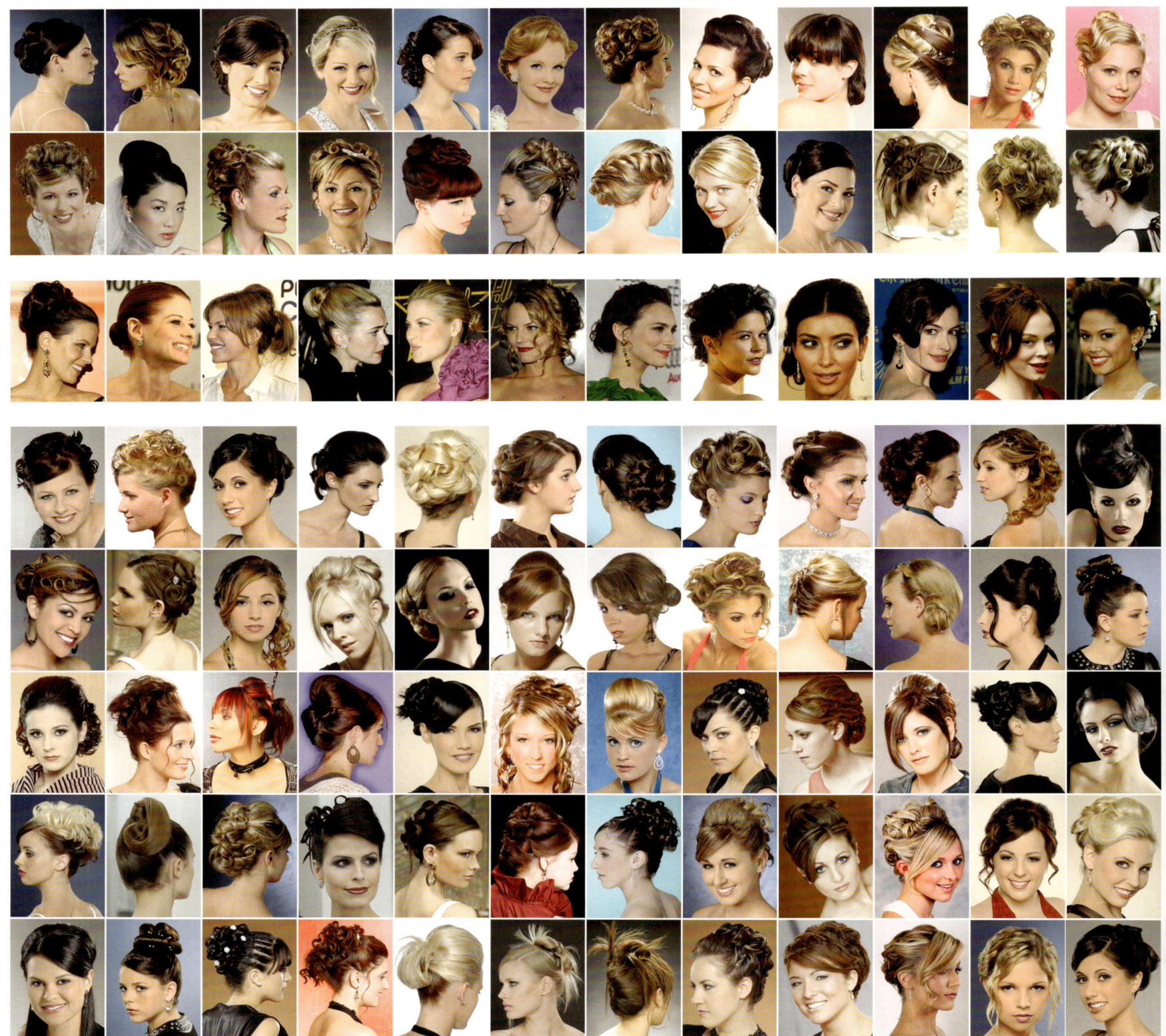

Table of Contents Volume 68

BRIDAL HAIR
2-25

CELEBRITY HAIR
26-33

UPSTYLES
34-96

HAIR: Pasquale Caselle
PHOTO: Michael Raveney

BRIDAL HAIR

Art of Hair
HAIR: Nicole Martin
MAKEUP: Jamie Queenin
PHOTO: Taggart Winterhalter
for Purely Visual

Elie Elie Salon
HAIR: Barbara Lhotan
MAKEUP: Linzie Wolford
PHOTO: Tom Carson

BRIDAL HAIR

Claiborne's Salon
HAIR: Claiborne's Design Team
MAKEUP: Claiborne's Design Team
PHOTO: Oma Cain

40-One Salon & Spa
HAIR: Maryann Jensen
MAKEUP: Matilda Lorenzo
PHOTO: Tom Carson

BRIDAL HAIR

Elie Elie Salon
HAIR: Barbara Lhotan
MAKEUP: Linzie Wolford
PHOTO: Tom Carson

Élan Hair Designs
HAIR: Penelopi Koutras
MAKEUP: Jeanette Beck
PHOTO: Michael McWeeney

Pave Nouveau
HAIR: Mandi Bevando
MAKEUP: Sara Wayne
PHOTO: Taggart Winterhalter
for Purely Visual

Salon Synergy
HAIR: Vicki Maki
MAKEUP: Jamie Queenin
PHOTO: Taggart Winterhalter for Purely Visual

BRIDAL HAIR

The Art of Hair Salon
HAIR: Grace Beckett
MAKEUP: Carlyn Phillips
PHOTO: Mike Renda

Diadema Hair Fashion
HAIR: Diadema
MAKEUP: Cristina Marzo per 20100Milano
PHOTO: Stefano Bidini

The Art of Hair Salon
HAIR: Jennifer Oakley
MAKEUP: Yamileth
PHOTO: Mike Renda

Elie Elie Salon
HAIR: Barbara Lhotan
MAKEUP: Linzie Wolford
PHOTO: Tom Carson

BRIDAL HAIR

Fantastic Sams-Temecula, CA
HAIR: Ryan DiGregorio
PHOTO: Taggart Winterhalter
for Purely Visual

HAIR: Daisy Sanchez
MAKE-UP: Daisy Sanchez
PHOTO: Orlando Perez Photography

BRIDAL HAIR

The Salon Professionals
HAIR: Stefanie Boaz
PHOTO: Tina VanDerhoof

Elie Elie Salon
HAIR: Barbara Lhotan
MAKEUP: Linzie Wolford
PHOTO: Tom Carson

BRIDAL HAIR

Elie Elie Salon
HAIR: Barbara Lhotan
MAKEUP: Linzie Wolford
PHOTO: Tom Carson

Style on 2nd
HAIR: Chris Vandehey
MAKEUP: Laura Kiny
PHOTO: Chris Ryan

BRIDAL HAIR

InStyle Salon
HAIR: Lisa Kapusinki
MAKEUP: Stephani Freidman
PHOTO: Drew Neerdaels

Updo's Studio
HAIR: Amanda Gatewood
MAKEUP: Heather Still
PHOTO: Still Shots Photography

Art of Hair
HAIR: Nicole Martin
MAKEUP: Sara Wayne
PHOTO: Taggart Winterhalter for Purely Visual

Updo's Studio
HAIR: Heather Still
MAKEUP: Amanda Gatewood
PHOTO: Still Shots Photography

BRIDAL HAIR

Sira 2000 Hair Salon
HAIR: Nena Perez
MAKEUP: Jaime Queenin
PHOTO: Taggart Winterhalter
for Purely Visual

Evolve Salon
HAIR: Kara Sullivan
MAKEUP: Sara Wayne
PHOTO: Taggart Winterhalter
for Purely Visual

BRIDAL HAIR

PON International
HAIR: Kathy Reed
MAKEUP: Jaime Queenin
PHOTO: Taggart Winterhalter for Purely Visual

Fantastic Sams - La Verne, CA
HAIR: Vanessa Grisham
PHOTO: Taggart Winterhalter
for Purely Visual

Fantastic Sams - Wildomar, CA
HAIR: Ryan Digregorio
PHOTO: Taggart Winterhalter
for Purely Visual

40-One Salon & Spa
HAIR: Virginia Karandrikas
MAKEUP: Matilda Lorenzo
PHOTO: Tom Carson

Tribeca Color Salon
HAIR: Amanda Stine
MAKEUP: Jen Wright
PHOTO: Ross Krison

BRIDAL HAIR

Amy Adams
PHOTO: Frank Micelotta/Getty Images

Jo Champa
PHOTO: Frank Micelotta/Getty Images

Catherine Zeta-Jones
PHOTO: Charley Gallay/Getty Images

CELEBRITY HAIR

Jessica Alba
PHOTO: Frank Micelotta/
Getty Images

Anne Hathaway
PHOTO: Jamie McCarthy/WireImage

Kim Kardashian
PHOTO: Gustavo Caballero/
Getty Images

Kim Kardashian
PHOTO: Gustavo Caballero/
Getty Images

CELEBRITY HAIR

Kate Winslet
PHOTO: Cory Schwartz/Getty Images

Jennifer Morrison
PHOTO: Andrew H. Walker/Getty Images

Debra Messing
PHOTO: Stephen Lovekin/Getty Images

Nikki Cox
PHOTO: Kevin Winter/Getty Images

Keira Knightley
PHOTO: Frank Micelotta/Getty Images

Charlize Theron
PHOTO: Frank Micelotta/Getty Images

America Ferrera
PHOTO: Stephen Lovekin/ Getty Images

Felicity Huffman
PHOTO: Frazer Harrison/ Getty Images

Loni Anderson
PHOTO: John Heller/
WireImage

Vanessa Minnillo
PHOTO: Frazer Harrison/
Getty Images

Maggie Gyllenhaal
PHOTO: Frazer Harrison/
Getty Images

Rachel Weiss
PHOTO: Frazer Harrison/
Getty Images

CELEBRITY HAIR

Kate Beckensdale
PHOTO: Stephen Lovekin/
Getty Images

Liane Balabah
PHOTO: Frazer Harrison/
Getty Images

Melissa Bent
PHOTO: Andrew H. Walker/Getty Images

CELEBRITY HAIR

Eva Longoria Parker
PHOTO: Frank Micelotta/Getty Images

Rose McGowan
PHOTO: Matt Carr/Getty Images

Marissa Tomei
PHOTO: Frederick M. Brown/Getty Images

élon Salon
HAIR: Flonnie Westbrook
COLOR: Flonnie Westbrook
MAKEUP: Fawn/Mac
PHOTO: Scott Bryant
Art Direction by
Larry Oskin &
The Marketing
Solutions Team

Pivot Point International, Inc.
HAIR: Elsa Haroldsdottir - Iceland,
Angelina Pasquet - Belgium,
Joakim Roos - Sweeden,
Tulio Talia - Italy,
Martin Wentstel - Netherlands,
Pascal Viton - France
MAKEUP: Carla Rep
PHOTO: Rob Peetoom

UPSTYLES

Fantastic Sams - Temecula, CA
HAIR: Ryan DiGregorio
PHOTO: Taggart Winterhalter for Purely Visual

Vincent Michael Salon
HAIR: Caitlyn Long
MAKEUP: Jaime Queenin
PHOTO: Taggart Winterhalter for Purely Visual

UPSTYLES

Carter T. Lund and Associates
HAIR: Carter T. Lund
MAKEUP: Sara Wayne
PHOTO: Taggart Winterhalter
for Purely Visual

Edie's Styling Center
HAIR: Lili Casanova
COLOR: Lili Casanova
MAKEUP: Lili Casanova
PHOTO: Scott Bryant
Art Direction by
Larry Oskin &
The Marketing
Solutions Team

UPSTYLES

Pivot Point International, Inc.
HAIR: Elsa Haroldsdottir - Iceland, Angelina Pasquet - Belgium, Joakim Roos - Sweeden, Tulio Talia - Italy, Martin Wentstel - Netherlands, Pascal Viton - France
MAKEUP: Carla Rep
PHOTO: Rob Peetoom

The David Salon-Costa Mesa, CA
HAIR: Brie Mulkern
MAKEUP: Sheryl Bell
PHOTO: Taggart Winterhalter for Purely Visual

Fantastic Sams - Costa Mesa, CA
HAIR: Leslie Escobar
PHOTO: Taggart Winterhalter for Purely Visual

American Hair
HAIR: Haley Kenyon
PHOTO: Robert Holmes, Shooting Stars

UPSTYLES

Michael Angelo Salon & Spa
HAIR: Jamie Savage
MAKEUP: Jenna Thompson
PHOTO: Michael Razzo

Claibornés Salon
HAIR: Claibornés Design Team
MAKEUP: Claibornés Design Team
PHOTO: Oma Cain

Calista Grand Salon
HAIR: Michelle Martin
MAKEUP: Jess Berryman/Kate Ray
PHOTO: Jack Cutler

UPSTYLES

Diadema Hair Fashion
HAIR: I Fuoriclasse
EXTENTION: Zeropiu
MAKEUP: 20100Milano
PHOTO: Stefano Bidini

UPSTYLES

Beverly Hills One of Alexandria
HAIR: Ken Smith
MAKEUP: Yen Mai & Dan Fores
PHOTO: Tom Carson

Art of Hair
HAIR: Robin Dunn
MAKEUP: Sara Wayne
PHOTO: Taggart Winterhalter
for Purely Visual

Fantastic Sams - Mira Loma, CA
HAIR: Magadelena Luevano
PHOTO: Taggart Winterhalter for Purely Visual

UPSTYLES

**John Amico Haircare & Jalyd Haircolor-
Shears To You, Oak Lawn, IL**
HAIR: Jennifer Macha
COLOR: Jennifer Macha
MAKEUP: Jennifer Macha
PHOTO: Scott Bryant
Art Direction by
Larry Oskin &
The Marketing
Solutions Team

47

Elie Elie Salon
HAIR: Barbara Lhotan
MAKEUP: Linzie Wolford
PHOTO: Tom Carson

ENJOY Hair Care
HAIR: Vincent Michael
COLOR: Oliver Zammit
MAKEUP: Jaime Queenin
PHOTO: Taggart Winterhalter
for Purely Visual

Fantastic Sams - Lake Elsinore, CA
HAIR: Rosalia Gauna
PHOTO: Taggart Winterhalter
for Purely Visual

UPSTYLES

Calista Grand Salon
HAIR: Heather Marie Seltzer
MAKEUP: Jackie Hashem
PHOTO: Jack Cutler

Calista Grand Salon
HAIR: Dayna Castilli
MAKEUP: Jackie Giovanisci
PHOTO: Jack Cutler

Claibornés Salon
HAIR: Claibornés Design Team
MAKEUP: Claibornés Design Team
PHOTO: Oma Cain

UPSTYLES

Beverly Hills One of Alexandria
HAIR: Jeffery Cuellar
MAKEUP: Yen Mai & Dan Forest
PHOTO: Tom Carson

UPSTYLES

Calista Grand Salon
HAIR: Alicia McLaughlin
MAKEUP: Jackie Giovanisci
PHOTO: Jack Cutler

Calista Grand Salon
HAIR: Heather Marie Seltzer
MAKEUP: Jackie Hashem
PHOTO: Jack Cutler

Calista Grand Salon
HAIR: Katie McCafferty
MAKEUP: Jess Berryman
PHOTO: Jack Cutler

The Art of Hair Salon
HAIR: Dawn Zick
MAKEUP: Carlyn Phillips
PHOTO: Mike Renda

Yellow Strawberry Salon
HAIR: Yellow Strawberry Salon Design Team
MAKEUP: Danielle Heredia
PHOTO: Tom Carson

Fantastic Sams - Huntington Beach, CA
HAIR: Jennifer Newman
PHOTO: Taggart Winterhalter
for Purely Visual

Salon Secrets Spa & Wellness Retreat
HAIR: Stephanie Nicole Pannell
COLOR: Stephanie Nicole Pannell
MAKEUP: Stephanie Nicole Pannell
PHOTO: Scott Bryant
Art Direction by Larry Oskin
& The Marketing
Solutions Team

Edie's Styling Center
HAIR: Lili Casanova
COLOR: Lili Casanova
MAKEUP: Lili Casanova
PHOTO: Scott Bryant
Art Direction by Larry Oskin
& The Marketing
Solutions Team

UPSTYLES

Art of Hair
HAIR: Nicole Martin
MAKEUP: Sara Wayne
PHOTO: Taggart Winterhalter for Purely Visual

Edie's Styling Center
HAIR: Lili Casanova
COLOR: Lili Casanova
MAKEUP: Lili Casanova
PHOTO: Scott Bryant
Art Direction by Larry Oskin & The Marketing Solutions Team

UPSTYLES

Julian Hans Salon
HAIR: Tara Rakowski
MAKEUP: Sara Wayne
PHOTO: Taggart Winterhalter
for Purely Visual

Fantastic Sams - Riverside, CA
HAIR: Rosie Garcilazo
PHOTO: Taggart Winterhalter
for Purely Visual

UPSTYLES

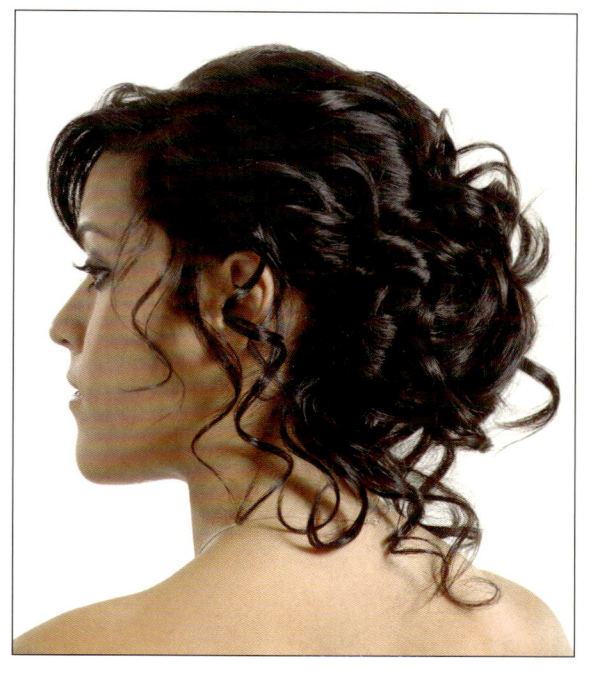

PON International
HAIR: Kathy Reed
MAKEUP: Jaime Queenin
PHOTO: Taggart Winterhalter for Purely Visual

Oak Street Hair Group
HAIR: Karin Peron
MAKEUP: Angela Jones
PHOTO: Tom Carson

**John Amico Haircare & Jalyd Haircolor-
Avalon Salon & Spa, Deer Park, FL**
HAIR: Jennifer Blanas
COLOR: Jennifer Blanas
MAKEUP: Diana Benjamin
PHOTO: Scott Bryant
Art Direction by Larry Oskin &
The Marketing Solutions Team

**Fantastic Sams -
Foothill Ranch, CA**
HAIR: Charles Holderman
PHOTO: Taggart Winterhalter
for Purely Visual

UPSTYLES

Claibornés
HAIR: Claibornés Design Team
MAKEUP: Claibornés Design Team
PHOTO: Oma Cain

Fantastic Sams - Tustin Ranch, CA
HAIR: Vera Melkumyan
PHOTO: Taggart Winterhalter
for Purely Visual

Salon Secrets Spa & Wellness Retreat
HAIR: Jennifer Vargason
COLOR: Jennifer Vargason
MAKEUP: Kim Lancashire
PHOTO: Scott Bryant
Art Direction by Larry Oskin
& The Marketing
Solutions Team

Salon Secrets Spa & Wellness Retreat
HAIR: Dianna Fraim
COLOR: Dianna Fraim
MAKEUP: Dianna Fraim
PHOTO: Scott Bryant
Art Direction by Larry Oskin
& The Marketing
Solutions Team

UPSTYLES

Fantastic Sams - Upland, CA
HAIR: Jennifer Martin
PHOTO: Taggart Winterhalter
for Purely Visual

Above and Beyond Salon
HAIR: Antonio Morosi
COLOR: Laura Hall
MAKEUP: Laura Hall
PHOTO: Tom Carson

M. Constantino Salon
HAIR: Janae Perkins
MAKEUP: Janae Perkins
PHOTO: Calvin Perkins/Perkins Photography

UPSTYLES

Claibornés Salon
HAIR: Claibornés Design Team
MAKEUP: Claibornés Design Team
PHOTO: Oma Cain

Fantastic Sams - Long Beach, CA
HAIR: Bertha Martinez
PHOTO: Taggart Winterhalter
for Purely Visual

Fantastic Sams – Huntington Beach, CA
HAIR: Margarita Zamora
PHOTO: Taggart Winterhalter
for Purely Visual

Salon Secrets Spa & Wellness Retreat
HAIR: Meg Steen
COLOR: Meg Steen
MAKEUP: Stephanie Burns
PHOTO: Scott Bryant
Art Direction by Larry Oskin
& The Marketing Solutions Team

Diadema Hair Fashion
HAIR: Diadema
MAKEUP: 20100 Milano
PHOTO: Stefano Bidini

Oak Street Hair Group
HAIR: Lori Egea
MAKEUP: Jestina Howard
PHOTO: Tom Carson

Purely Visual
HAIR: Tracy Guthrie
MAKEUP: Anastacia
PHOTO: Taggart Winterhalter
for Purely Visual

UPSTYLES

Fantastic Sams - Norco, CA
HAIR: Linda Morrell
PHOTO: Taggart Winterhalter
for Purely Visual

ENJOY Hair Care
HAIR: Donny Anderson
COLOR: Quenya Pollakoff
MAKEUP: Jaime Queenin
PHOTO: Taggart Winterhalter
for Purely Visual

Images: 126 Salon
HAIR: Christy Casey
MAKEUP: Christy Casey
PHOTO: Kasey VanScyoc

Gadabout Salon
HAIR: Todd Bozoich
MAKEUP: Mary Miller
PHOTO: "Adrian"
Courtesy of Intercoiffure

UPSTYLES

The Brown Aveda Institute
HAIR: Allie Purdy
PHOTO: Tom Carson

Purely Visual
HAIR: Tracy Guthrie
MAKEUP: Anastacia
PHOTO: Taggart Winterhalter
for Purely Visual

UPSTYLES

Fantastic Sams - Corona, CA
HAIR: Magda Nieblas-Zapien
PHOTO: Taggart Winterhalter
for Purely Visual

Art of Hair
HAIR: Robin Dunn
MAKEUP: Jaime Queenin
PHOTO: Taggart Winterhalter
for Purely Visual

PON International
HAIR: Tayja Avila
MAKEUP: Sara Wayne
PHOTO: Taggart Winterhalter
for Purely Visual

UPSTYLES

Grand Avenue Salon
HAIR: Manuel Mora
MAKEUP: Sara Wayne
PHOTO: Taggart Winterhalter
for Purely Visual

Oak Street Hair Group
HAIR: William Winslett
MAKEUP: Angela Jones
PHOTO: Tom Carson

Salon Adesso
HAIR: RaNae Kimmel Mendiola
MAKEUP: Jaime Queenin
PHOTO: Taggart Winterhalter
for Purely Visual

UPSTYLES

Pivot Point International, Inc.
HAIR: Elsa Haroldsdottir -Iceland, Angelina Pasquet- Belgium, Joakim Roos - Sweeden, Tulio Talia - Italy, Martin Wentstel - Netherlands, Pascal Viton - France
MAKEUP: Carla Rep
PHOTO: Rob Peetoom

UPSTYLES

Pivot Point International, Inc.
HAIR: Elsa Haroldsdottir -Iceland, Angelina Pasquet- Belgium, Joakim Roos - Sweeden, Tulio Talia - Italy, Martin Wentstel - Netherlands, Pascal Viton - France
MAKEUP: Carla Rep
PHOTO: Rob Peetoom

Pivot Point International, Inc.
HAIR: Elsa Haroldsdottir -Iceland, Angelina Pasquet- Belgium, Joakim Rocs - Sweeden, Tulio Talia - Italy, Martin Wentstel - Netherlands, Pascal Viton - France
MAKEUP: Carla Rep
PHOTO: Rob Peetoom

40-One Salon & Spa
HAIR: Maryann Jensen
MAKEUP: Matilda Lorenzo
PHOTO: Tom Carson

UPSTYLES

Carter T. Lund and Associates
HAIR: Carter T. Lund
MAKEUP: Jaime Queenin
PHOTO: Taggart Winterhalter
for Purely Visual

Beauty Brands
HAIR: Kim Metcalf
PHOTO: Susanne DeLong

Evolve Salon
HAIR: Kara Sullivan
MAKEUP: Jaime Queenin
PHOTO: Taggart Winterhalter for Purely Visual

UPSTYLES

Calista Grand Salon
HAIR: Erin Lazos
PHOTO: Jack Cutler

The Art of Hair Salon
HAIR: Dawn Zick
MAKEUP: Carlyn Phillips
PHOTO: Mike Renda

85

Carter T. Lund and Associates
HAIR: Charlene Galindo
MAKEUP: Jaime Queenin
PHOTO: Taggart Winterhalter
for Purely Visual

Tribeca Color Salon
HAIR: Amanda Stine
MAKEUP: Jen Wright
PHOTO: Ross Krison

Rico's Downtown Salon
HAIR: Snooky Rico
MAKEUP: Jaime Queenin
PHOTO: Taggart Winterhalter for Purely Visual

Fantastic Sams - Corona, CA
HAIR: Rosalia Guana
PHOTO: Taggart Winterhalter for Purely Visual

UPSTYLES

**John Amico Haircare & Jalyd Haircolor-
Jan Michaels Salon & Spa, Worth, IL**
HAIR: Candace Marusarz
COLOR: Candace Marusarz
MAKEUP: Gina McIver
PHOTO: Scott Bryant
Art Direction by
Larry Oskin
& The Marketing
Solutions Team

40-One Salon & Spa
HAIR: Michelle Natale
MAKEUP: Matilda Lorenzo
PHOTO: Tom Carson

UPSTYLES

Fantastic Sams - Corona, CA
HAIR: Rosalia Guana
PHOTO: Taggart Winterhalter for Purely Visual

New Wave Salons
HAIR: Cindy Carrone
PHOTO: Robert Holmes, Shooting Stars

John Amico Haircare & Jalyd Haircolor-CP Directions Studio, Morton, IL
HAIR: Carol A. Paluska
COLOR: Carol A. Paluska
MAKEUP: Carol A. Paluska
PHOTO: Scott Bryant
Art Direction by Larry Oskin & The Marketing Solutions Team

John Amico Haircare & Jalyd Haircolor- Paula's Design Team
HAIR: Paula Boldman
COLOR: Paula Boldman
MAKEUP: Brandy Long
PHOTO: Scott Bryant
Art Direction by Larry Oskin & The Marketing Solutions Team

Diadema Hair Fashion
HAIR: Diadema
MAKEUP: 20100 Milano
PHOTO: Stefano Bidini

UPSTYLES

Indiana's Premier Hair Academy
HAIR: Ashley Johnson
COLOR: Ashley Johnson
MAKEUP: Ashley Johnson
PHOTO: Scott Bryant
Art Direction by Larry Oskin
& The Marketing Solutions Team

UPSTYLES

Salon Secrets Spa & Wellness Retreat
HAIR: Meg Steen
COLOR: Meg Steen
MAKEUP: Stephanie Burns
PHOTO: Scott Bryant
Art Direction by Larry Oskin
& The Marketing Solutions Team

John Amico Haircare & Jalyd Haircolor- Paula's Design Team
HAIR: Eric Williams
COLOR: Eric Williams
MAKEUP: Eric Williams
PHOTO: Scott Bryant
Art Direction by Larry Oskin
& The Marketing Solutions Team

Fantastic Sams - Corona, CA
HAIR: Karina Cortez
PHOTO: Taggart Winterhalter
for Purely Visual

Hair Benders Internationalé - Chattanooga, TN
HAIR: Hair Benders Design Team
COLOR: Hair Benders Design Team
MAKEUP: Darin Wright
PHOTO: Scott Bryant
Art Direction by Larry Oskin & The Marketing Solutions Team

UPSTYLES

Roberts Salon & Day Spa, Greenwood, IN
HAIR: Bea Wagoner
MAKEUP: Ella Hattery
PHOTO: Scott Bryant
Art Direction by Larry Oskin & The Marketing Solutions Team

Purely Visual
HAIR: Tracy Guthrie
MAKEUP: Anastacia
PHOTO: Taggart Winterhalter for Purely Visual

INDEX VOLUME SIXTY EIGHT

Salon	Photograher	Page
40-One Salon & Spa	Tom Carson	6,25,82,88
Above and Beyond Salon	Tom Carson	65
American Hair	Robert Holmes, Shooting Stars	40
Art of Hair	Taggart Winterhalter for Purely Visual	3,20,46,58,76
Beauty Brands	Susanne DeLong	84
Beverly Hills One of Alexandria	Tom Carson	45,52
Calista Grand Salon	Jack Cutler	43,50,53,54,85
Carter T. Lund and Associates	Taggart Winterhalter for Purely Visual	37,83,86
Claiborne's Salon	Oma Cain	5,42,51,63,67
Daisy Sanchez	Orlando Perez Photography	14
Diadema Hair Fashion	Stefano Bidini	9,11,44,69,91
Edie's Styling Center	Scott Bryant	38,57,59
Elan Hair Designs	Michael McWeeney	7
Elie Elie Salon	Tom Carson	4,7,12,16,17,48
élon Salon	Scott Bryant	34
ENJOY Hair Care	Taggart Winterhalte for Purely Visual	49,71
Evolve Salon	Taggart Winterhalter for Purely Visual	22,84
Fantastic Sams - Corona, CA	Taggart Winterhalter for Purely Visual	75,87,89,94
Fantastic Sams - Costa Mesa,CA	Taggart Winterhalter for Purely Visual	40
Fantastic Sams - Foothill Ranch,CA	Taggart Winterhalter for Purely Visual	62
Fantastic Sams - Huntington Beach,CA	Taggart Winterhalter for Purely Visual	56,68
Fantastic Sams - Lake Elsinore,CA	Taggart Winterhalter for Purely Visual	49
Fantastic Sams - Long Beach,CA	Taggart Winterhalter for Purely Visual	67
Fantastic Sams - Mira Loma,CA	Taggart Winterhalter for Purely Visual	47
Fantastic Sams - Norco,CA	Taggart Winterhalter for Purely Visual	71
Fantastic Sams - Riverside,CA	Taggart Winterhalter for Purely Visual	60
Fantastic Sams - Tustin Ranch,CA	Taggart Winterhalter for Purely Visual	63
Fantastic Sams - Upland,CA	Taggart Winterhalter for Purely Visual	65
Fantastic Sams- La Verne,CA	Taggart Winterhalter for Purely Visual	24
Fantastic Sams- Temecula,CA	Taggart Winterhalter for Purely Visual	13,36
Fantastic Sams- Wildomar,CA	Taggart Winterhalter for Purely Visual	24
*Gadabout Salon	"Adrian"	72
	Getty Images, Frank Micelotta	26,28,30,33
	Getty Images, Charley Gallay	27
	Getty Images, Gustavo Cabellero	28
	Getty Images, Cory Schwartz	29
	Getty Images, Andrew H. Walker	29,32
	Getty Images, Stephen Lovekin	29,30,32
	Getty Images, Kevin Winter	29
	Getty Images, Frazer Harrison	30,31,32
	Getty Images, Matt Carr	33
	Getty Images, Frederick M.Brown	33
Grand Avenue Salon	Taggart Winterhalter for Purely Visual	77
Hair Benders Internationalé	Scott Bryant	94
Images: 126 Salon	Kasey VanScyoc	72
Indiana's Premier Hair Academy	Scott Bryant	92
InStyle Salon	Drew Neerdaels	19
John Amico Haircare & Jalyd Haircolor - Avalon Salon	Scott Bryant	62
John Amico Haircare & Jalyd Haircolor - CP Directions Studio	Scott Bryant	90
John Amico Haircare & Jalyd Haircolor - Jan Michaels Salon & Spa	Scott Bryant	88
John Amico Haircare & Jalyd Haircolor - Paula's Design Team	Scott Bryant	90,93
John Amico Haircare & Jalyd Haircolor - Shears to You	Scott Bryant	47
Julian Hans Salon	Taggart Winterhalter for Purely Visual	60
M. Constantino Salon	Calvin Perkins/Perkins Photography	66
Michael Angelo Salon & Spa	Michael Razzo	41
New Wave Salon	Robert Holmes, Shooting Stars	89
Oak Street Hair Group	Tom Carson	61,70,78
Pasquale Caselle	Michale Raveney	2
Pave Nouveau	Taggart Winterhalter for Purely Visual	8
Pivot Point International,Inc.	Rob Peetroom	35,39,80,81
PON International	Taggart Winterhalter for Purely Visual	23,61,76
Purely Visual	Taggart Winterhalter for Purely Visual	70,74,96
Rico's Downtown Salon	Taggart Winterhalter for Purely Visual	87
Roberts Salon & Day Spa	Scott Bryant	95
Salon Adesso	Taggart Winterhalter for Purely Visual	79
Salon Secrets Spa & Wellness Retreat	Scott Bryant	56,64,68,93
Salon Synergy	Taggart Winterhalter for Purely Visual	10
Sira 2000 Hair Salon	Taggart Winterhalter for Purely Visual	21
Style on 2nd	Chris Ryan	18
The Art of Hair Salon	Mike Renda	11,12,54,85
The Brown Aveda Institute	Tom Carson	73
The David Salon - Costa Mesa,CA	Taggart Winterhalter for Purely Visual	39
The Salon Professionals	Tina VanDerhoof	15
Tribeca Color Salon	Ross Krison	25,86
Updo's Studio	Still Shots Photography	19,20
Vincent Michael Salon	Taggart Winterhalter for Purely Visual	36
	WireImage, Jamie McCarthy	28
	WireImage, John Heller	31
Yellow Strawberry Salon	Tom Carson	55

*Courtesy of Intercoiffure

Publisher/CEO: Deborah Carver • Managing Director: Sheryl Lenzkes • Art Director: Michael Block • Photo Coordinator: Hannah Ross
To Contact Us: Creative Age Communications • 7628 Densmore Avenue, Van Nuys, California 91406-2042 • PH 800.634.8500 • FAX 818.782.7450
Interested in getting published . . . go to inspirebooks.com to download submission forms and information